20 Christmas Carols For Solo Clarinet Book 1

Michael Shaw

Copyright © 2015 Michael Shaw. All rights reserved. Including the right to reproduce this book or portions thereof, in any form. No part of this text may be reproduced in any form without the express written permission of the author.

Music Arrangements. All Christmas Carol arrangements in this book by **Michael Shaw Copyright © 2015**

ISBN: 1516945891
ISBN-13: 978-1516945894

www.mikesmusicroom.co.uk

Contents

Introduction	
I Saw Three Ships	1
Auld Lang Syne	2
Away In A Manger	3
O Come All Ye Faithful	4
Deck The Halls	5
Ding Dong Merrily On High	6
The First Noel	7
God Rest Ye, Merry Gentlemen	8
Hark The Herald Angels Sing	9
The Holly And The Ivy	10
Joy To The World	11
Jingle Bells	12
Good King Wenceslas	14
O Christmas Tree	15
Once In Royal David's City	16
While Shepherds Watched Their Flocks	17
Silent Night	18
What Child Is This?	19
We Three Kings	20
We Wish You A Merry Christmas	22
About The Author	24

Introduction

The Christmas sheet music in this book has been arranged for easy solo Clarinet.

You can also play together in a duet or ensemble with other instruments with a book for that instrument. To get a book for an instrument other than your own, choose from the 20 Christmas Carols Series Book 1. All arrangements are the same and keys are adjusted for B flat, E flat, F and C instruments so everything sounds correct. Instruments in this series include Tenor Saxophone, Oboe, French Horn, Trumpet, Trombone and Flute. Please check out my author page on Amazon to view these books.

Author Page US
amazon.com/Michael-Shaw/e/B00FNVFJGQ/

Author Page UK
amazon.co.uk/Michael-Shaw/e/B00FNVFJGQ/

I Saw Three Ships

Clarinet

William Sandys

Auld Lang Syne
Clarinet

Scotland

Clarinet in B♭

Away In A Manger
Clarinet

Traditional

Clarinet in B♭

O Come All Ye Faithful
Clarinet
John Francis Wade

Deck The Halls

Clarinet

Traditional

Ding Dong Merrily On High

Clarinet

Unknown French

The First Noel
Clarinet
Traditional

God Rest Ye Merry Gentlemen

Clarinet

Traditional

Hark The Herald Angels Sing

Clarinet

Mendelssohn

The Holly And The Ivy
Clarinet

Traditional

Joy To The World
Clarinet

Lowell Mason

Jingle Bells

Clarinet

James Pierpoint

Good King Wenceslas
Clarinet
Traditional

O Christmas Tree

Clarinet

German

Once In Royal David's City

Clarinet

Henry John Gauntlett

While Shepherds Watched Their Flocks
Clarinet

Traditional

Silent Night
Clarinet

Traditional

What Child Is This?
Clarinet

Traditional

We Three Kings

Clarinet

John H. Hopkins

We Wish You A Merry Christmas

Clarinet

Traditional

About the Author

Mike works as a professional musician and keyboard music teacher. Mike has been teaching piano, electronic keyboard and electric organ for over thirty years and as a keyboard player worked in many night clubs and entertainment venues.

Mike has also branched out in to composing music and has written and recorded many new royalty free tracks which are used worldwide in TV, film and internet media applications. Mike is also proud of the fact that many of his students have gone on to be musicians, composers and teachers in their own right.

You can connect with Mike at:

Facebook
facebook.com/keyboardsheetmusic

Soundcloud
soundcloud.com/audiomichaeld

YouTube
youtube.com/user/pianolessonsguru

I hope this book has helped you with your music, if you have received value from it in any way, then I'd like to ask you for a favour: would you be kind enough to leave a review for this book on Amazon? It'd be greatly appreciated!

Thank You
Michael Shaw

Made in United States
Troutdale, OR
11/14/2023

14588227R00018